BATSFORD'S

London's Kings and Queens

Malcolm Day

BATSFORD

Early history

London has had a chequered history as a capital city. The Romans built Londinium in AD 50 and it became a thriving centre because of its good strategic position for trade with Continental Europe. It was nevertheless always subject to attack. Boudicca, queen of the British Celts, rebelled against Roman control and sacked the city with ease in AD 61. London's vulnerability led the Romans to build a defensive wall (London Wall) in about AD 200. It followed a crooked line, forming an arc from today's Tower of London area to the mouth of the River Fleet, enclosing more than the built-up area. Fragments of the wall remain, marking the old City of London boundary. This area is also known today as London's 'Square Mile'.

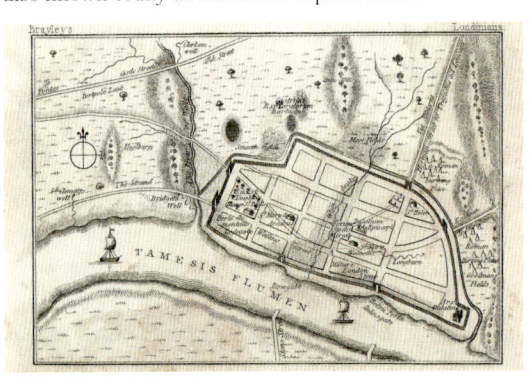

Boudicca, queen of the Celts

Roman Londinium with its grid of straight roads

Part of the Roman wall of London

King Canute proclaimed London to be capital of all England in 1016

The nave of Westminster Abbey

Saxons and Danes

After the Romans withdrew, the city fell prey to intermittent attacks from various raiding peoples. Viking longboats frequently pushed up the River Thames during the eighth and ninth centuries, the Vikings burning and looting wherever they went. The Saxon King Alfred recovered the smouldering wreck of the city in the ninth century, turning it once again into a thriving centre. The Saxons also laid down the basic street pattern of what is today's City of London, albeit overlaid with subsequent developments, and it was they who started the expansion west with a ribbon development below today's Strand. Because of London's continuing vulnerability to Viking raids, Winchester, at a safe distance from the coast, was the seat of rule until the Danish King Canute proclaimed London to be capital of all England in 1016.

Palace of Westminster

Following the westward trend set by earlier Saxons, the seat of government moved from the City to Westminster. Upon a patch of hard ground known as Thorney Island, now the site of the Houses of Parliament, King Canute built a palace in the eleventh century. From here, Edward the Confessor, who was crowned king in 1042, watched his dream come true as a modest Saxon church nearby was turned into a magnificent abbey like those he had witnessed while exiled in Normandy. This was Westminster Abbey, and it was consecrated just days before the king's death in 1066.

The dome of St Paul's

St Paul's Cathedral

During the Roman occupation, Christianity was just one of many different cults practised in London. The faith proper did not establish itself here until the seventh century, when King Ethelbert founded St Paul's Cathedral as the focus of worship. But fire was a constant hazard in the timbered city, and the cathedral fell prey to it four times. Ethelbert's building was destroyed in 961; its replacement, designated the royal burial ground, burned down in 1087. A hastily built Norman cathedral was severely damaged in 1221, a much grander edifice was designed in the traditional shape of a cross, together with the huge spire often depicted in medieval manuscripts. This building survived until the Great Fire of London in 1666, after which it was the turn of Christopher Wren to produce the domed St Paul's we have today (see Christopher Wren, page 25).

The Norman Conquest

When the Normans invaded England in 1066, the land would suffer yet another occupying force, only this time its leader, William of Normandy, promised a benign rule: '... all the burghers within London, French and English [be] friendlike. And I will that both be worthy of all the rights of which ye both were worthy in King Edward's day.'

English monarchs 1066–1485

The Normans (1066–1154)
William I (William the Conqueror) 1066–1087
William II (William Rufus) 1087–1100
Henry I 1100–1135
Stephen and Matilda 1135–1154

The Angevins (1154–1216)
Henry II 1154–1189
Richard I (Richard the Lionheart) 1189–1199
John I 1199–1216

The Plantagenets (1216–1399)
Henry III 1216–1272
Edward I 1272–1307
Edward II 1307–1327
Edward III 1327–1377 (father of Edward, the Black Prince, 1330–1376, who died before he could be crowned king)
Richard II 1377–1399 (son of the Black Prince)

The House of Lancaster (1399–1461)
Henry IV 1399–1413
Henry V 1413–1422
Henry VI 1422–1461, 1470–1471

The House of York (1461–1485)
Edward IV 1461–1470, 1471–1483
Edward V 1483
Richard III 1483–1485

Rather than blast his way in, the French duke took the more civilized course of surrounding the city until its leaders were forced, by a shortage of food, to capitulate. So on Christmas Day 1066, they crowned him King William I of England over the grave of Edward the Confessor in Westminster Abbey.

The triumphant William the Conqueror enters London

The Crown jewels

Of the several elements that make up the Crown jewels of today – crowns, sceptres, orbs, swords – the core structure is known as St Edward's Crown, after Edward the Confessor. Although it had to be reconstructed after Oliver Cromwell (see page 14) melted down the Crown jewels, this crown has been lowered on to the heads of successive monarchs since Edward the Confessor's coronation in 1043. The sapphire at the centre of the ensemble is said to have been one of Edward's rings, and the Black Prince's ruby was worn by Henry V on his helmet during the Battle of Agincourt. Most of the Crown jewels are kept in the Tower of London, guarded by Yeomen Warders, also known as Beefeaters.

> **St Edward's Crown has been lowered on to the heads of successive monarchs since 1043**

A Yeoman of the Guard

The four-turreted White Tower

The Tower of London

Though declaring peaceful intentions, William took no chances with his fierce Saxon subjects and set about building strongholds by which to defend the capital if need be. Three were erected at strategic points of the London Wall; the only one to survive was also the most prominent – the Tower of London, built at the eastern end of the wall overlooking the Thames. The immensity of the central keep – the four-turreted White Tower (so named after its white stone, brought over from Caen in France) – was intended not only to deter attack, but also to impress on the inhabitants the might of their new overlord. Massive walls, 30 m (90 ft) high were, and still are, a formidable sight.

The Tower of London in Elizabethan times

Prisoners were beheaded on Tower Green, inside the curtain wall

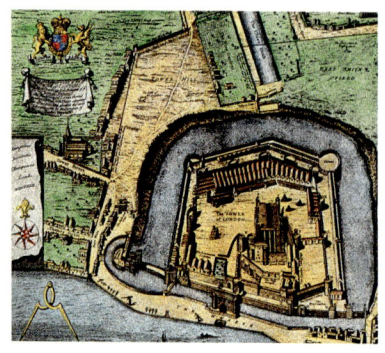

Lady Jane Grey is beseeched to take the crown

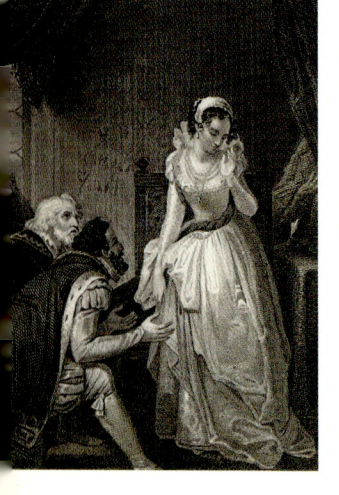

A home and a prison

The keep contained living apartments for the royal family and household, and an austere chapel dedicated to St John. The king still retained the Palace of Westminster as his main residence and used the Tower for refuge in times of crisis (as did Richard II during the Peasants' Revolt). Later kings added various outlying features that have survived. Henry III was responsible for most of the inner curtain wall and defensive towers, of which the most famous is the 'Bloody Tower'. Here, prisoners of state were held pending trial. The tower gets its nickname from the supposed murder of the two sons of Edward IV, the Princes in the Tower, in 1483.

Prisoners were brought by boat to Traitors' Gate – through which passed Sir Thomas More (d. 1535) and Lady Jane Grey (d. 1554) to be executed on Tower Hill. Aristocratic victims, such as Anne Boleyn (d. c. 1536) and Catherine Howard (d. 1542), wives of Henry VIII, were beheaded on Tower Green, inside the curtain wall.

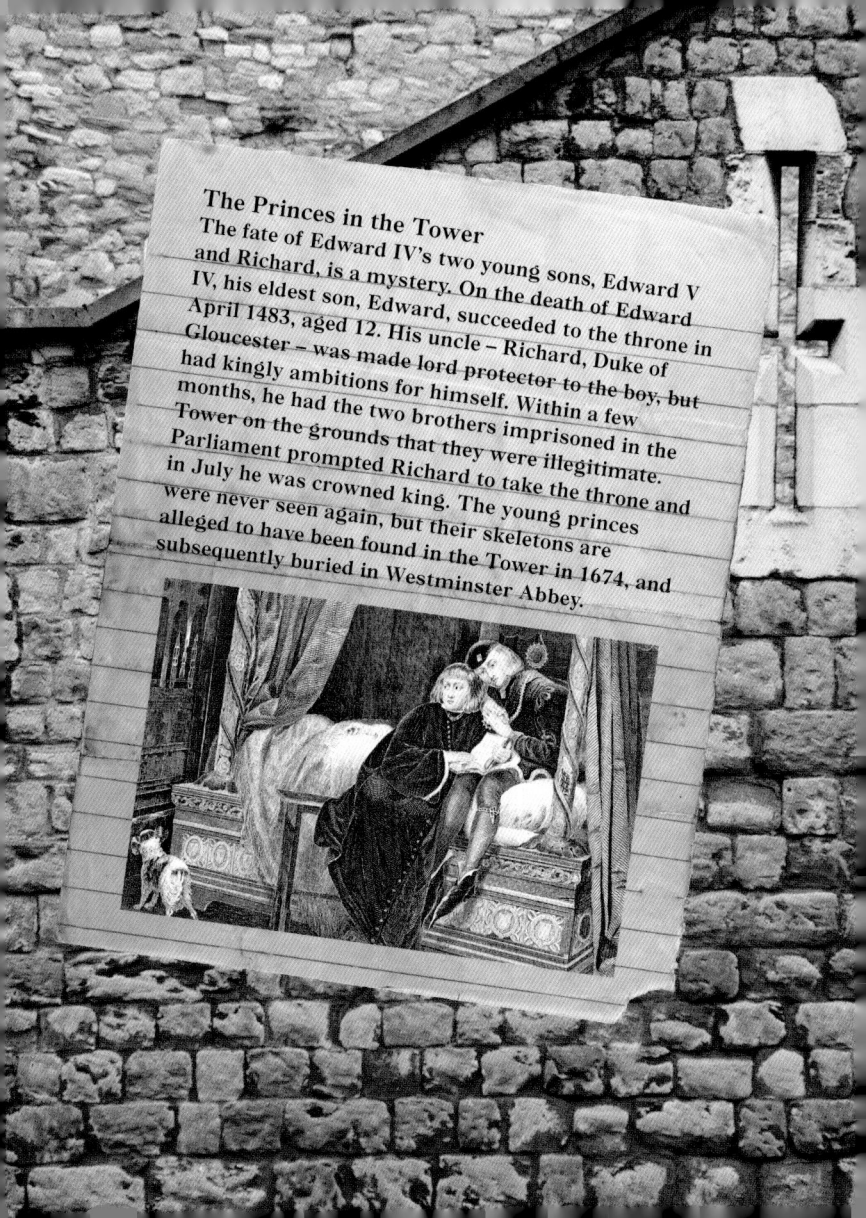

The Princes in the Tower

The fate of Edward IV's two young sons, Edward V and Richard, is a mystery. On the death of Edward IV, his eldest son, Edward, succeeded to the throne in April 1483, aged 12. His uncle – Richard, Duke of Gloucester – was made lord protector to the boy, but had kingly ambitions for himself. Within a few months, he had the two brothers imprisoned in the Tower on the grounds that they were illegitimate. Parliament prompted Richard to take the throne and in July he was crowned king. The young princes were never seen again, but their skeletons are alleged to have been found in the Tower in 1674, and subsequently buried in Westminster Abbey.

Windsor Castle

Another of William the Conqueror's strongholds was Windsor Castle, located 48 km (30 miles) west of London. It was one of several military bases to form a defensive ring around London. Not until the reign of Henry II was the place used as a royal residence. Nothing remains of the original wooden building, a classic motte-and-bailey fortification.

Rebuilding and restoration

Successive monarchs have made their mark on Windsor. Henry II built the first stone Round Tower, but this was replaced in the thirteenth century in an extensive rebuilding programme by Henry III. Edward IV began building the Chapel of St George, the resting place of ten monarchs. After the Wars of the Roses, when the realm became inwardly more secure, modifications to the castle reflected a greater emphasis on its role as palace rather than fortification. More consideration was given to comfort for monarchs, who regarded this remote retreat as a safe haven.

The castle suffered during the Civil War, when Oliver Cromwell used it as his principal military base. So it fell to Charles II, during the Restoration of the monarchy, to begin its refurbishment. Following the baroque style of Versailles, near Paris, he commissioned the elaborate banqueting room, St George's Hall (though this was toned down in the next century) and the Long Walk, a tree-lined avenue running for 5 km (3 miles). Despite his embellishments, successive sovereigns preferred to live elsewhere; until, that is, George III needed a large residence to house his 15 children and so made Windsor his main home.

It was his extravagant son, George IV, who probably made more changes to Windsor than any other monarch. The accumulation, over the centuries, of random features was brought into a symmetrical whole, largely in Gothic style. The Round Tower was raised to its present height, giving it a commanding presence visible from afar. The final appearance is a mix of the medieval and late Gothic, as you would expect of a castle converted into a palace.

English monarchs 1485–1603

The Tudors (1485–1603)
Henry VII 1485–1509
Henry VIII 1509–1547
Edward VI 1547–1553
Lady Jane Grey 1553
Mary I (Bloody Mary) 1553–1558
Elizabeth I 1558–1603

United Kingdom monarchs 1603–1901

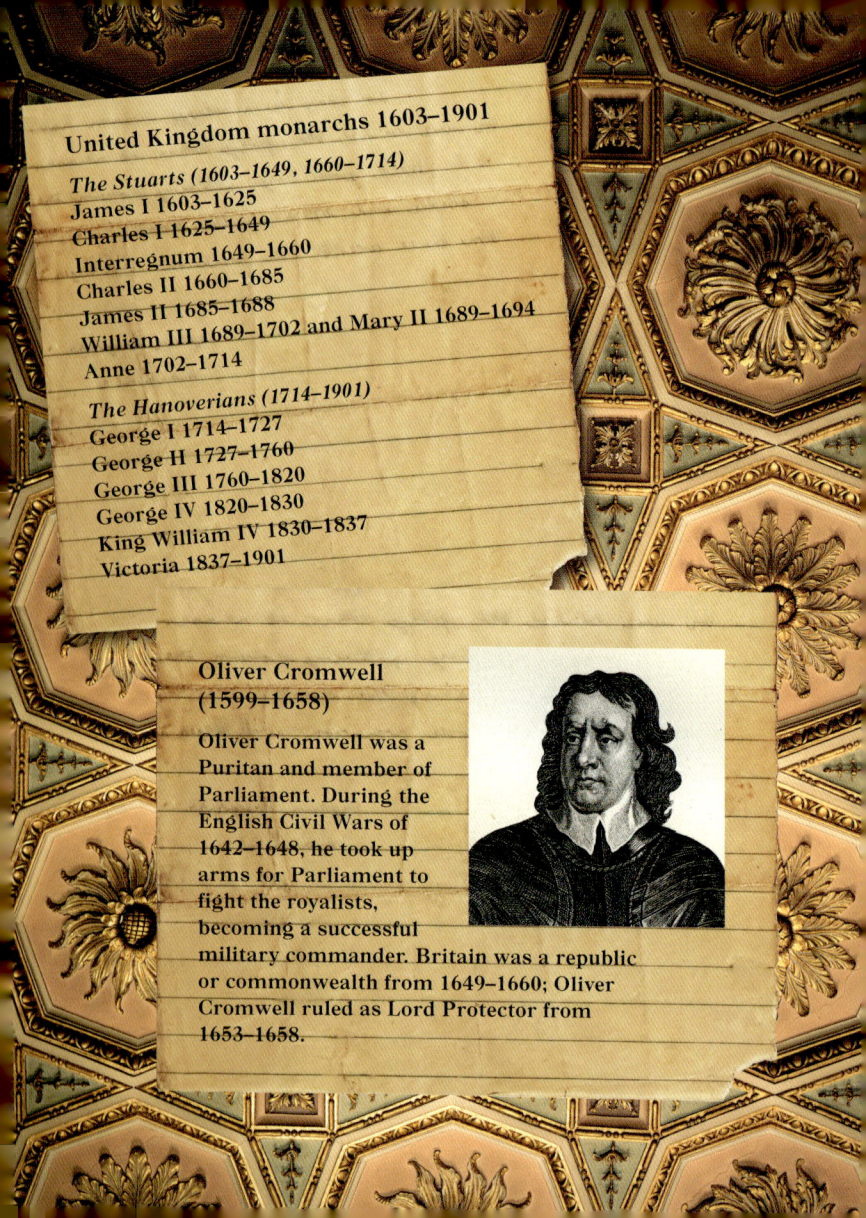

The Stuarts (1603–1649, 1660–1714)
James I 1603–1625
Charles I 1625–1649
Interregnum 1649–1660
Charles II 1660–1685
James II 1685–1688
William III 1689–1702 and Mary II 1689–1694
Anne 1702–1714

The Hanoverians (1714–1901)
George I 1714–1727
George II 1727–1760
George III 1760–1820
George IV 1820–1830
King William IV 1830–1837
Victoria 1837–1901

Oliver Cromwell (1599–1658)

Oliver Cromwell was a Puritan and member of Parliament. During the English Civil Wars of 1642–1648, he took up arms for Parliament to fight the royalists, becoming a successful military commander. Britain was a republic or commonwealth from 1649–1660; Oliver Cromwell ruled as Lord Protector from 1653–1658.

Great Fire of 1992

A fire that began in the Queen's private chapel in November 1992 spread fast and furiously for the better part of a day before being extinguished. Nine state rooms were destroyed and many more badly damaged. An extensive restoration programme, involving some 1,500 architects and craftsmen, managed to renovate virtually everything in five years. Determined that the public should not bear any of the cost involved, the Queen launched an annual opening of Buckingham Palace to paying visitors to help cover the £37 million bill.

The 1992 fire of Windsor Castle

Order of the Garter

The highest and oldest honour of the realm is known as the Most Noble Order of the Garter. Founded by Edward III in the fourteenth century, the knighthood may be bestowed only by the sovereign, and 'at the sovereign's pleasure'. Membership of the Order of the Garter is limited to 24 Companions, plus royalty and officers. The origin of the name is disputed. One account holds that when, at a medieval banquet, a lady's garter fell embarrassingly down her leg, King Edward III picked it up and placed it around his thigh, exclaiming, '*Honi soit qui mal y pense*' (Shamed be the person who thinks evil of it). The utterance has become the motto of the Order. Members include military and business personnel, and politicians such as the former prime ministers Baroness Margaret Thatcher and Sir John Major. The Order of the Garter ceremony takes place at Windsor Castle.

The Queen uses Windsor Castle both as a home and for official duties; parts of it are also open to the public

Badge of the Order of the Garter

Heritage of the Tudors

The wool trade brought great prosperity to England in the Middle Ages, and the Tudor monarchs were direct beneficiaries through taxation. Both Henry VII and Henry VIII were keen builders. From Hampton Court Palace to the shipyards of the East End, the 'king's works' could be seen dotted along the River Thames.

Richmond Palace

Before Henry VIII embarked upon his great building spree, his father, Henry VII, is known to have created a palace upriver of London. The king liked to spend time at Sheen Palace, dating from the twelfth century. Not long after his accession to the throne, it burned down and he had it replaced in 1499. He called the new palace Richmond Palace, after the town in Yorkshire where he held an earldom. Both Henry VIII and Elizabeth I were born here. In 1625, Charles I relocated his court here to escape the plague and turned the grounds into a walled deer park. Nothing of the palace remains except the gateway.

The Richmond Palace gateway today

Hans Holbein's portrait of Henry VIII

Greenwich Palace

Henry VIII dances with Anne Boleyn at Greenwich

Greenwich and the East End

Vaulting west to east over the capital would take us to Greenwich, where Henry VIII and Elizabeth I had their favourite palace, Placentia, with its three quadrangles and hunting ground (now Greenwich Park). From its windows, Elizabeth hailed Martin Frobisher on his way to search for the North-West Passage to China, and Sir Francis Drake fired a salute to her on his return from sailing around the world. Its easterly remoteness meant that the palace gradually fell out of favour with later monarchs, and in its place was erected a naval hospital for returning war veterans.

Designed by Nicholas Hawksmoor and Christopher Wren, the institution consisted of two halves, each topped with the classic hallmark of Wren architecture, the elegant dome. Colonnaded inner flanks led the eye up to, but did not obscure the view from, the earlier Queen's House created by Inigo Jones. Since the nineteenth century, the naval hospital has been the base of the Royal Naval College.

Queen's House, Greenwich

Queen's House

Inigo Jones, who was court architect during the Stuart dynasty for over 20 years, introduced in his design for Queen's House the neoclassical Italianate style known as Palladian, which came to dominate British architecture. It was commissioned by James I in 1616 for his wife, Anne of Denmark, and was the first classical building in England. Unfortunately, Anne died before the house was completed in 1637. Its first occupant was the wife of Charles I, Henrietta Maria, who described it as her 'house of delights'.

Docklands

Intent on enlarging the navy for likely battles with France and Spain, Henry VIII built shipyards at Deptford and Woolwich, and on the north bank of the Thames at Poplar and Blackwall. Soon, the areas east of the Tower of London were filled with docks, creating the broad area known as the East End. The low class of its denizens was noted by one contemporary writer, who described numerous small cottages 'inhabited by sailors' victuallers'.

Palace of Whitehall

The government buildings of Whitehall now stand on the site of Whitehall Palace, developed largely by Henry VIII and his successors. Cardinal Wolsey began the work by taking York Place, the London residence of the Archbishop of York, and building the Great Hall, to be called 'White Hall', a hall for festivities.

Cardinal Wolsey

Banqueting House, Whitehall

Henry confiscated this building and all the land around it because he wished to link the riverside buildings with those facing St James's Park and keep the entire area for his own private use. The problem was that there was a public thoroughfare between Charing Cross, to the north, and Westminster. To get round this, he built a gatehouse known as the Holbein Gate (named after the painter Hans Holbein, who stayed there). It was designed with an arch that allowed the public to pass through. Although this gatehouse no longer exists, a similar sort of building can be seen today at St James's Palace, which Henry VIII also had built.

Fire!

The palace became the main residence of English monarchs in London until it burned down in 1698. It was less a unified building than a maze of courtyards and passageways, much as the offices of government are today. Charles II made some alterations, turning the Great Hall into a theatre, and building a chemistry laboratory and indoor tennis court. Alas, virtually all went up in flames after a laundry girl accidentally started a fire. Only the Banqueting House has survived. This elegant Italianate building, designed by Inigo Jones for James I in 1619, represented a significant advance on the prevailing Jacobean style. The ceiling was painted by Rubens.

Virtually all went up in flames after a laundry girl accidentally started a fire

The Rubens ceiling at Banqueting House

Hans Holbein: court painter

Henry VIII was a great patron of the arts, and had several court painters. His favourite was a German artist, Hans Holbein, whose portraits were renowned for their fine detail and true likenesses. Henry commissioned him to paint portraits of his wives. Indeed, the standard of these was so good that the king once dispatched Holbein to Europe to paint a prospective wife, Anne of Cleves. Ironically, having accepted the girl as his bride on the evidence of the painting, Henry was disappointed on meeting the princess, denouncing her as a 'Flanders Mare'.

The gatehouse at St James's Palace

St James's Palace
Another royal residence built by Henry VIII was St James's Palace, at the end of Pall Mall. Using the site of a former leper hospital dedicated to St James the Less, the palace was constructed in the classic Tudor red brick. The most striking feature to survive is the gatehouse, with its battlemented turrets. Though not favoured as a primary residence by monarchs until Queen Anne came to the throne in 1702, it did then remain the chief royal residence until Victoria's accession in 1837 – she preferred Buckingham Palace. Even today, foreign ambassadors are officially accredited as 'Ambassador to the Court of St James's'. The palace buildings are now the London residence of members of the royal family, and provide offices for servants of the Crown.

Clarence House (built 1825), next to St James's Palace, is the official residence of Prince Charles and Princes William and Harry

St James's Park and Pall Mall

To the west of Whitehall lay St James's Park, which was once a marsh, but Henry VIII had it drained to create a recreation ground. The Stuart kings developed the park to enhance their daily promenades. James I added the Royal Aviary, a menagerie of exotic birds, which has given rise to Birdcage Walk on the south side. Following the style of the gardens at Versailles, Charles II had the long ornamental lake dug.

A French game similar to croquet was introduced at some point, involving a long alley (777m/ 850 yd), balls, mallets and a hoop at each end. The English called the game 'pell-mell' (from *palla*, ball, and *maille*, mallet), hence the name of the street now called Pall Mall, where the game was originally played outside St James's Palace. It was later moved into the quieter environment of St James's Park. To avoid confusion with its former site, the new alley was named simply The Mall.

The street called Pall Mall takes its name from a game

Hampton Court Palace

Like St James's Palace, Hampton Court was built at great expense in Tudor red brick, laid in diaper (diamond) fashion. It is the sole Tudor palace near London to have survived. It is situated south-west of London in East Molesey, next to the River Thames.

Hampton Court Palace

Archbishop's palace

Designed by Cardinal Wolsey, the Archbishop of York and chancellor, as a sumptuous riverside country mansion, the palace has all the hallmarks of grand Tudor style, with its distinctive militaristic parapets and turrets, gatehouse and ornamented chimneys. No expense was spared in Wolsey's outrageous specifications. There were a thousand rooms hung with fine tapestries, and nearly 300 silken beds to accommodate visiting kings and queens and their retinues. To ensure the utmost hygiene, he laid 4.8 km (3 miles) of lead pipes to bring water: not from the River Thames, which might be contaminated, but from pure springs. Needless to say, Henry became somewhat envious of his subject's unique passion and took it over when the archbishop fell out of favour.

> **There were 1,000 rooms hung with fine tapestries, and nearly 300 silken beds to accommodate visiting kings and queens and their retinues**

Henry VIII extends

The king added new wings and courtyards, and being more of a sportsman than the cardinal, built tennis courts, a bowling alley and a tilting yard for royal jousts – in which he was a keen participant.

The palace was further developed in the next century by Christopher Wren, who was commissioned by William and Mary to replace some of the Tudor buildings with apartments in the baroque style. The joint monarchs also redesigned the grounds to create the formal Fountain Garden, with yew-lined avenues fanning out below the Queen's Drawing Room. A great vine and maze are other features of the palace.

Architect Sir Christopher Wren

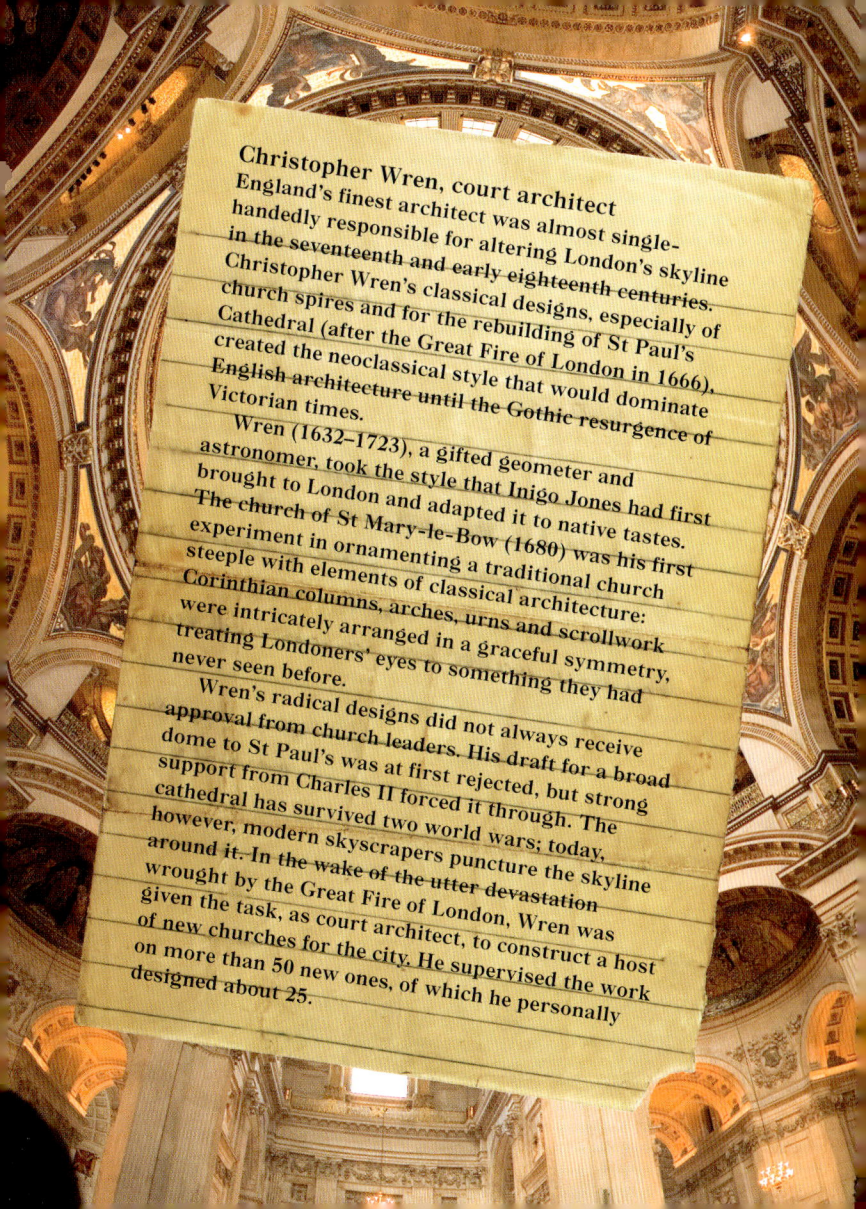

Christopher Wren, court architect

England's finest architect was almost single-handedly responsible for altering London's skyline in the seventeenth and early eighteenth centuries. Christopher Wren's classical designs, especially of church spires and for the rebuilding of St Paul's Cathedral (after the Great Fire of London in 1666), created the neoclassical style that would dominate English architecture until the Gothic resurgence of Victorian times.

Wren (1632–1723), a gifted geometer and astronomer, took the style that Inigo Jones had first brought to London and adapted it to native tastes. The church of St Mary-le-Bow (1680) was his first experiment in ornamenting a traditional church steeple with elements of classical architecture: Corinthian columns, arches, urns and scrollwork were intricately arranged in a graceful symmetry, treating Londoners' eyes to something they had never seen before.

Wren's radical designs did not always receive approval from church leaders. His draft for a broad dome to St Paul's was at first rejected, but strong support from Charles II forced it through. The cathedral has survived two world wars; today, however, modern skyscrapers puncture the skyline around it. In the wake of the utter devastation wrought by the Great Fire of London, Wren was given the task, as court architect, to construct a host of new churches for the city. He supervised the work on more than 50 new ones, of which he personally designed about 25.

Kensington Palace

Kensington Palace

When Mary II processed up the Thames from Greenwich to join William of Orange in a joint monarchy, she was expecting to move into the palace in which she grew up – Whitehall – before her father James II was forced to flee into exile. But William wished for somewhere quiet, away from the water (which he said gave him asthma), yet not far from the hub of the capital. He bought a modest house in Kensington and commissioned Wren to alter and extend it to their needs. Thus was created Kensington Palace.

The south front looks today almost exactly as it did in Wren's day

The south front looks today almost exactly as it did in Wren's day, with the King's Gallery overlooking an ornamental garden. Tragically, within a few years of its completion, Mary died of smallpox, aged 32. And eight years later, her husband died there after a riding accident. Its next incumbent, Queen Anne, followed the fashion of the time by creating a more exotic feel, with an orangery and extensive ornamental gardens.

The Serpentine and Hyde Park

Queen Caroline, wife of George II, considerably improved the recreational possibilities by creating the 'Long Water'. Now known as the Serpentine, it was then just a tract of marsh and pond fed by the West Bourne, a tributary of the Thames; its conversion allowed royals to use it for sailing and bathing. The Serpentine separates Kensington Gardens from Hyde Park, once the private hunting ground of Henry VIII. Charles I created a carriage drive called the Ring and opened Hyde Park to the public so they could admire aristocrats at play, horse-racing and duelling. The park was the site of the Great Exhibition of 1851, for which the grand Crystal Palace was erected. Latterly, it has become a place for large-scale demonstrations.

Once Buckingham Palace had become the chief royal residence for George III in 1762, Kensington Palace was used only occasionally, and by royal relatives. Queen Victoria was born there; perhaps its most famous resident was Princess Diana.

Hyde Park

**Monarchs of the United Kingdom
1901–present**

House of Saxe-Coburg-Gotha (1901–1910)
Edward VII 1901–1910

House of Windsor (1910–present)
George V 1910–1936
Edward VIII 1936
George VI 1936–1952
Elizabeth II 1952–present

Buckingham Palace

The present home and official headquarters of Queen Elizabeth II is a grand state building, more in keeping with serious government affairs than regal opulence. However, the present austere frontage is a twentieth-century overlay of several earlier designs. A Georgian building of 1705, made for the first Duke of Buckingham, was called Buckingham House. This enchanting mansion, with classical columns and a baroque fountain, was bought by George III in 1762 as a private residence for Queen Charlotte, and became known as the Queen's House. The king lived at St James's Palace.

Buckingham House pictured in 1714

Buckingham Palace

Nash's redesign

By this time, the sovereign had a very different set of duties from those of earlier dynasties. He or she no longer had to preside over ministerial meetings in a 'cabinet' adjoining the bedroom. Power had been wrested into the hands of Parliament and became for the monarch largely symbolic. Now somewhere was needed for lavish state balls and for entertaining visiting heads of state; a balcony from which to receive applause from the public was also required. The house was not grand enough for these purposes, so in the 1820s, the Regency architect John Nash was brought in to convert it into a palace for George IV. His redesign created large, beautiful apartments on the first floor around an open quadrangle, and there was a marble arch at the entrance. Unfortunately, the arch was too narrow to accommodate state carriages, so the whole structure had to be moved to its present site at the corner of Hyde Park.

> **Power had been wrested into the hands of Parliament and became for the monarch largely symbolic**

Queen Elizabeth II with Prince Philip after her coronation in 1953

The modern era

Further alterations were made for Victoria, including a vast ballroom, and for George V, who commissioned Aston Webb to reface the front in 1913. The wide processional avenue, The Mall, and triumphal Admiralty Arch, at one end, were Edwardian embellishments intended to vaunt Britain's imperial status.

> There are 775 rooms in Buckingham Palace, including 19 staterooms, 52 royal and guest bedrooms, and 78 bathrooms

The fire at Windsor Castle in 1992 prompted the Queen to open the staterooms of Buckingham Palace to the public in the summer. The Queen's Gallery houses her collection of paintings. Every summer, she invites guests from all walks of life to a tea party held in the 40 acres of palace gardens.

Today the Princess Royal (Anne), Prince Andrew and Prince Edward all have apartments in Buckingham Palace; Prince Charles has his London home at Clarence House.

The annual garden party held at Buckingham Palace

Admiralty Arch

Trooping the Colour

Every June, the Queen leaves Buckingham Palace to drive down The Mall in her carriage to Horse Guards Parade, where she will inspect some 500 members of the household division – the troops in charge of guarding the royal family. This parade was originally intended to show troops the 'colour', or flag, of their regiment so it would be recognized on the battlefield. Today, only one colour is trooped each year. The five regiments of foot guards – Coldstreams, Grenadiers, Welsh, Irish and Scots Guards – take it in turns to troop their colour.

The 19th century

One of the most extraordinary periods in the history of English royalty was the era known as the Regency, when the Prince Regent (son of George III; the future George IV) held power in the king's absence due to prolonged illness from 1811–1820. Famous for his extravagant lifestyle, the Prince of Wales started out as a popular man. Tall, handsome, witty and intelligent, he became known as 'the first gentleman of Europe'. But in time, a penchant for excess, in part to irritate his father, led him to react to the dull orthodoxy of restrained Georgiana and add some flamboyance to everything he encountered – including architecture. Thus was born Regency style. To this end, he appointed John Nash as his court architect.

A cartoon by Gilray of the Prince Regent

Nash and the Regent

Together, Nash and the Prince Regent restyled the West End of London. This area had become the fashionable centre of the Georgian era. Grand homes went up along Piccadilly and Pall Mall, and new residential squares were developed at St James's, Bloomsbury, Cavendish, Hanover, Leicester Fields, Soho and Bedford Square. Lord Grosvenor expanded his estate to 100 acres in Mayfair. All formed a neat, if monotonous, alignment.

Regent Street pictured in 1848

Then, in a burst of creativity, the Nash–Regent partnership cut a swathe through the area, known as the Nash Sweep (now Regent Street), connecting the Prince Regent's intended home at Carlton House in St James's with the elegant villas and terraces of Nash's newly created Regent's Park. The scheme invented the Circus, most famously Piccadilly Circus (later adorned by the statue of Eros).

Together, Nash and the Prince Regent restyled the West End of London

Towards the end of his life, Nash laid plans for Trafalgar Square to adjoin Carlton House Terrace, but died before they could be implemented and Charles Barry completed his vision. Nash also had a big hand in reshaping Buckingham Palace, which the prince decided would be his home in preference for Carlton House, subsequently abandoned.

Cumberland Terrace

Cumberland Terrace

Some say that Nash's crowning achievement was Cumberland Terrace in Regent's Park. Conceived to be visible from the Prince of Wales's residence at Carlton House, the terrace occupies a prominent position, with elegant drawing rooms raised to the first floor opening out on to a terrace overlooking the park. Its broad, neoclassical front, with Ionic columns surmounted by a pediment decorated with classical figures, recalls the Parthenon in Athens.

Regent's Park

An integral part of the Nash redevelopment scheme was his vision of Regent's Park. Formerly Marylebone Park, a Tudor hunting ground, the area was planned by Nash to provide recreation for the Prince Regent, who had become George IV by the time the park was opened in 1835. There was an artificial lake, a zoo, an open-air theatre and a rose garden. Regent's Zoo was probably the most ambitious scheme, supplemented by species brought from collections at the Tower Menagerie and Windsor Castle.

However, the garden city that Nash envisioned never fully materialized. Many more villas were planned than built. His idea of running a canal through the park also foundered, on the grounds that it might be dangerous and noisome for genteel residents. Nevertheless, his Regent's Canal successfully linked the west of London with Limehouse Docks in the east via the Grand Union Canal.

The Ranger's House

In 1798 Queen Caroline, the estranged wife of the Prince Regent, was forced to leave court and set up home elsewhere. She chose the Ranger's House in Greenwich Park, suitably distant from the hurly-burly of state life. Here, in an elegant red-brick house with balustraded parapet, she lived for 16 years in a relaxed atmosphere, learning to play the harp and piano, and even tending her own vegetable garden.

Covent Garden

One positive impact of Henry VIII's Dissolution of the Monasteries was the subsequent development of a convent garden, used by monks attached to Westminster Abbey. In the seventeenth century the Earl of Bedford, who owned the land, commissioned the architect Inigo Jones to design London's first square. It was modelled on an Italian piazza, flanked by colonnaded townhouses built in the Palladian style.

Soon a market established itself for selling fruit, vegetables and flowers; artists and actors were attracted to the area, which led in turn to the building of the Covent Garden Theatre in the eighteenth century and the Royal Opera House in the Victorian era.

Covent Garden at Christmas

The Victoria and Albert Museum

Victoria and Albert

Three years after acceding to the throne in 1837, Queen Victoria married her German cousin Prince Albert. Over the course of their 21-year union she allowed him increasingly to take initiatives, and it is he who we have to thank for many of London's cultural landmarks. Albert recognised that British design and research could not match that of their European rivals. To encourage the arts and sciences he developed Kensington into an area of museums and learned societies.

His first major project was the successful Great Exhibition of 1851, held in Hyde Park in a specially erected glass emporium, dubbed the 'Crystal Palace' by Punch magazine. Originally publicised as 'the Works of Industry of all Nations', its primary purpose was in fact to showcase Britain's industrial skills and achievements. This event became the springboard for a permanent exhibition space designed a year later, the Victoria and Albert Museum. Galleries display sculpture, furniture, fashion trends, textiles, ceramics and jewellery from all over the world. A few years later land was bought nearby on which to erect the Natural History Museum, one of the world's finest collections of historical animals and fossils.

In memory of her late husband, and in honour of his patronage of the arts and sciences, Queen Victoria commissioned two major constructions. The first was the Albert Memorial in Kensington Gardens (pictured on page 1). The ornate 55-metre high statue has a gilded canopy with Venetian mosaics and glass stones, and marble carvings depicting artists, musicians and writers of the world. A few years later she laid the foundation stone for a grand concert hall, the Royal Albert Hall. This magnificent red and gold amphitheatre now famously stages the Promenade Concerts ('the Proms') every summer.

Victoria and Albert open the Great Exhibition

The Royals today

Power oozed from the kings and queens of old England. Their subjects quaked before them, as royal whim was mightier than the law. But gradually, as Parliament wrested this power, the law assumed the role of supreme arbiter in the land, and the importance of royalty diminished. Today, the Royals have essentially become ceremonial functionaries. Although, for example, Parliament must receive the Queen's blessing of its proposals for the forthcoming term of government, her role is little more than to rubber-stamp them.

The customs of pageantry and state occasions have their roots steeped in cherished tradition

Nevertheless, the nation maintains a pride in keeping the customs of pageantry and state occasions that have their roots steeped in cherished tradition. As representatives of Britain at the highest level, members of the Royal Family symbolize an approval from on high, whether it is marking an official opening, a national commemoration or an award of honour for outstanding achievement. It is perhaps no surprise that together the Royal Family patronises over 3,000 charities in Britain, of which about 600 come under the personal aegis of the Queen.

Patronage
As a result of some questioning of the monarchy's role in the recent past, the Royals have responded by expanding the range and depth of their involvement in charitable works. Usually, their support is offered for causes for which they feel some personal concern or interest. Prince Charles, for example, is a strong supporter of environmental preservation. When plans

for a new wing to the National Gallery were revealed in 1991, the Prince stepped in amid much protest to quash the design, calling it 'a monstrous carbuncle on the face of a much-loved friend'. Its replacement was also criticized for being a wishy-washy compromise.

> **Prince Charles is a strong supporter of environmental preservation**

His son and heir, Prince William, is patron of the Centrepoint charity, which helps care for the homeless. The Princess Royal (as Princess Anne is now known), one-time member of the equestrian eventing team in the Montreal Olympics, now feeds her passion for the sport by helping to direct the organization of the London Olympics in 2012.

Prince Charles and Camilla, Duchess of Cornwall

The Royal Variety Performance

In support of entertainers who have fallen upon hard times, whether through old age, poor health or poverty, the Royal Variety Performance is staged once a year. The proceeds of the event are donated to Brinsworth House, Twickenham, the nursing home for retired members of the entertainment profession. The occasion dates to 1912 when the present Queen's grandparents, King George V and Queen Mary, attended a 'Royal Command Performance' at the Palace Theatre in Shaftesbury Avenue. As the title suggests, the evening is light-hearted and includes various acts: from cabaret and song to magic shows and the idiosyncratic.

Defender of the Realm

The historic duty of the head of state as Defender of the Realm means that one of the Queen's chief duties is as patron of the Royal British Legion. This organization provides support, financial and otherwise, for veterans of the armed forces, past and present. Each year on Remembrance Sunday (the nearest Sunday to Armistice Day, 11 November), the Queen heads the Commonwealth ceremony of laying wreaths at the cenotaph in Whitehall to commemorate the fallen in battle. Originally, this marked the end of the First World War at the eleventh hour on the eleventh day of the eleventh month of 1918. The occasion now remembers the dead of all subsequent wars.

Prince William with a wreath on Remembrance Sunday

Calendar of key royal events in London

• *May to July*
Changing of the guard at Buckingham Palace
Every day at 11.30 am, guards from the Queen's Guard change duty to the accompaniment of military music. The soldiers are drawn from one of five regiments of foot guards of the British Army. When the Queen is in residence, four sentries – dressed in the full uniform of red tunics and black bearskins – stand guard in the forecourt of the palace; when she is absent, just two are on duty.

Horse guard, Buckingham Palace

• *June*
Garter Day
Garter Day takes place on the Monday of Royal Ascot week (the famous horse-racing event). In a solemn ceremony held in the Throne Room at Windsor Castle, the Queen appoints new Companions of the chivalric Order of the Garter (see page 15). Founded by Edward III in 1348, the order is the most senior and oldest of the realm's orders of chivalry.

- *June*
Trooping the Colour
On the second Saturday of June, the splendid Trooping the Colour ceremony is the high point of the royal year in London. It also marks the official birthday of the monarch in power (Queen Elizabeth II's real birthday is on 21 April) with a special birthday parade. Over two or three evenings in the fortnight leading up to this pageant, bands of the Household Cavalry and foot guards perform the traditional Beating the Retreat ceremony at Horse Guards Parade.

- *October/November*
State Opening of Parliament by the Queen

The Royal Collection

For over 500 years, kings and queens have amassed collections of art and artefacts. Many of these items still exist today as part of the Royal Collection, the Royal Philatelic Collection, the Royal Archives and the Crown jewels. Many of the objects are on public display at the royal residences, including the Queen's Gallery at Buckingham Palace and the Drawings Gallery at Windsor Castle. The collection includes paintings, drawings and watercolours, furniture, ceramics, clocks, silver, sculpture, jewellery, books, manuscripts, prints and maps, arms and armour, fans and textiles.

Queen Elizabeth II at the State Opening of Parliament

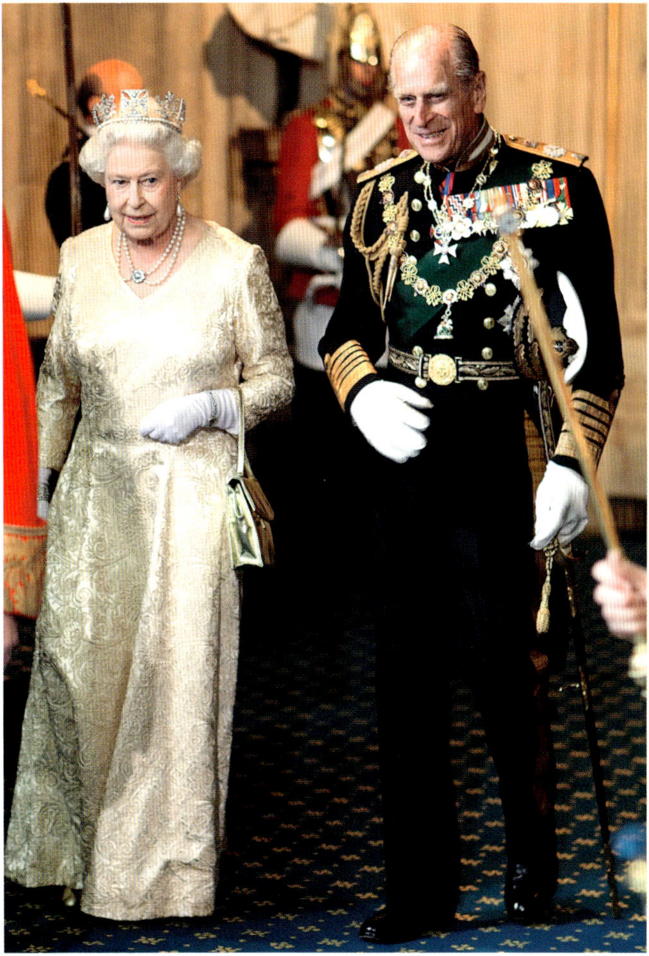

Princess Diana

A popular figure outside the royal family in her lifetime, Princess Diana will be remembered more for her clashes with senior royals, including her former husband, Prince Charles, than for the happier, early period of her marriage. Quite how much she was adored by the public may well have shocked this tragic figure, were she to have seen the immense outpouring of grief following her death in 1997. Princess Diana died in a car accident in Paris with her friend and lover, Dodi Al-Fayed.

Wreaths, of extraordinary number, were laid beside the railings surrounding Kensington palace and along adjacent roads. Over 32 million people in Britain watched the state funeral conducted in Westminster Abbey, the traditional burial site of royalty. Dubbed the 'People's Princess', memorials to her have been placed in the open grounds of Kensington Gardens, next to her beloved home, for all the public to see.

Her love of children – she was patroness of Great Ormond Street Hospital for Children – is reflected in the creation of a memorial playground, close to Kensington Palace. Inspired by the tale of Peter Pan, the playground is full of props to aid the imagination and sense of adventure.

The Princess of Wales, 1984

The Diana, Princess of Wales, Memorial Walk is a walkway (11 km/ 7 miles long) running through four of London's most beautiful parks: Kensington Gardens, Hyde Park, Green Park and St James's Park. Plaques are stationed along the way to indicate famous buildings and places associated with her life. These include the Italian Gardens in Hyde Park, Spencer House (once owned by her ancestors), St James's Palace, Buckingham Palace, the Albert Memorial, and of course her home at Kensington Palace.

Plaque to mark the Memorial Walk

An important legacy of Princess Diana was her influence in bringing about a worldwide ban on the use of landmines. Their deadliness, especially to innocent children unaware of the dangers, struck a chord with the princess, who undertook special fact-finding missions to the war-torn areas of Angola and Bosnia in 1997.

The Diana, Princess of Wales Memorial Fountain, Hyde Park

Sights to see

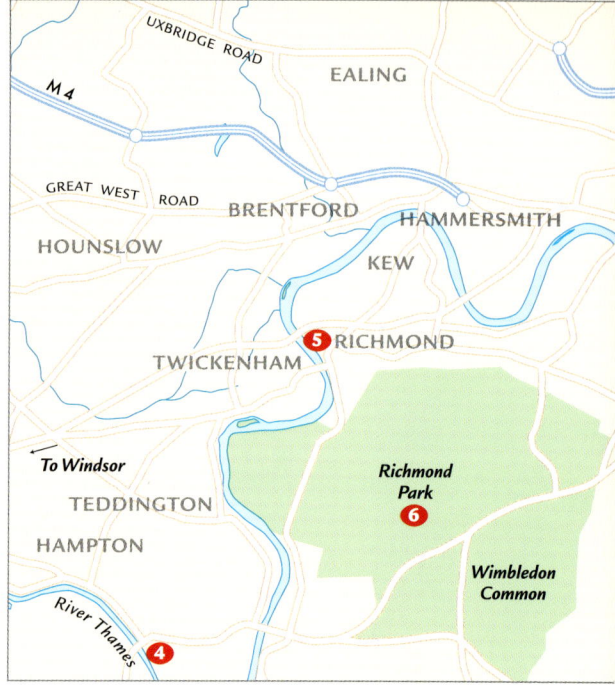

The map above shows some of the main sights covered in this book.

1. Westminster Abbey (page 4)
2 St Paul's Cathedral (page 5)
3 Tower of London (page 9)
4 Hampton Court (page 23)
5 Richmond Palace Gatehouse (page 16)
6 Richmond Park (page 16)
7 Queen's House, Greenwich (page 19)
8 Ranger's House, Greenwich (page 35)
9 Banqueting House, Whitehall (page 20)
10 St James's Palace (page 22)

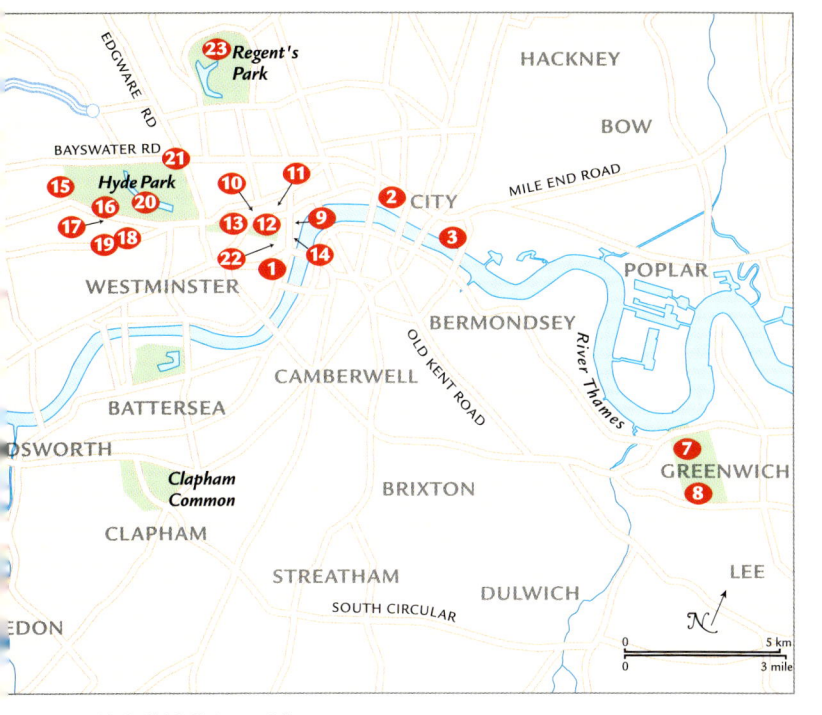

11 Pall Mall (page 23)
12 The Mall (page 23)
13 Buckingham Palace (page 28)
14 Palace of Westminster (page 4)
15 Kensington Palace and Gardens (page 26)
16 Albert Memorial, Kensington Gardens (page 37)
17 Royal Albert Hall (page 36)
18 Victoria and Albert Museum (page 36)
19 Natural History Museum (page 37)
20 Hyde Park (page 27)
21 Marble Arch (page 29)
22 Horse Guards Parade (page 31)
23 Regent's Park (page 34)

First published in the United Kingdom in 2011 by
Batsford, 10 Southcombe Street, London W14 0RA
An imprint of Anova Books Company Ltd

Copyright © Batsford 2011

All rights reserved. No part of this publication may be reproduced, stored in a retrieval system, or transmitted in any form or by any means, electronic, mechanical, photocopying, recording or otherwise, without the prior written permission of the copyright owner.

ISBN: 978 1 906388 96 6
A CIP catalogue record for this book is available from the British Library.

18 17 16 15 14 13 12 11
10 9 8 7 6 5 4 3 2 1

Reproduction by Rival Colour Ltd, UK
Printed by 1010 Printing Ltd, China

This book can be ordered direct from the publisher at the website www.anovabooks.co.uk, or try your local bookshop.

Picture credits

Page 1 © Tim Ayers Photography / Alamy; 2 (top and bottom) © Mary Evans Picture Library / Alamy ; 3 © Tim Jones / Alamy; 4 © North Wind Picture Archives / Alamy; 5 © Paul Pickard / Alamy; 7 © North Wind Picture Archives / Alamy; 8 © Amoret Tanner / Alamy; 9 © Tim Ayers Photography / Alamy; 10 (top) © North Wind Picture Archives / Alamy; (bottom) © Mary Evans Picture Library / Alamy; 11 (background) © Visualsafari Images / Alamy; (inset) © Classic Image / Alamy; 12–13 © Ivy Close Images / Alamy; 13 © Greg Balfour Evans / Alamy; 14 (background) © The National Trust Photolibrary / Alamy; (inset) © Lebrecht Music and Arts Photo Library / Alamy; 15 (top) © Martin Beddall / Alamy; (bottom) © Imagestate Media Partners Limited - Impact Photos / Alamy; 16 © Beata Moore / Alamy; 17 *Portrait of Henry VIII* (1491–1547), Holbein the Younger, Hans (1497/8–1543) / © Belvoir Castle, Leicestershire, UK / The Bridgeman Art Library ; 18 (top) © Mary Evans Picture Library / Alamy; (bottom) © 19th era / Alamy; 19 © Ben Ramos / Alamy; 20 (top) © Timewatch Images / Alamy; (bottom) © Elmtree Images / Alamy; 21 © Rolf Richardson / Alamy; 22 © Eric Nathan / Alamy; 23 © BANANA PANCAKE / Alamy; 24 © Lebrecht Music and Arts Photo Library / Alamy; 25 © John Norman / Alamy; 26 © one-image photography / Alamy; 27 © Kevin Allen / Alamy; 28 © Classic Image / Alamy; 29 © Jon Arnold Images Ltd / Alamy; 30 (top and bottom) © Pictorial Press Ltd / Alamy; 31 (top) © Tim Ayers Photography / Alamy; (bottom) © nobleIMAGES / Alamy; 32 © Lordprice Collection / Alamy; 33 © 19th era 2 / Alamy; 34 © Kirsty McLaren / Alamy; 35 (background) © The Art Archive / Alamy; (inset) © Jon Arnold Images Ltd / Alamy; 36 © John Farnham / Alamy; 37 © Mary Evans Picture Library / Alamy; 39 © London Red Carpet / Alamy; 40 © Trinity Mirror / Mirrorpix / Alamy; 41 © Keith Taylor / Alamy; 43 © newsphoto / Alamy; 44 © Pictorial Press Ltd / Alamy; 45 (top) © Dave Porter / Alamy; (bottom) © Colin Palmer Photography / Alamy. Map on page 46 courtesy of Martin Brown Design